MATHS
BOOSTER
Teacher's guide

Scholastic Education, an imprint of Scholastic Ltd

Book End, Range Road, Witney, Oxfordshire, OX29 0YD

Registered office: Westfield Road, Southam, Warwickshire, CV47 0RA

www.scholastic.co.uk

© 2017, Scholastic Ltd

1 2 3 4 5 6 7 8 9   7 8 9 0 1 2 3 4 5 6

British Library Cataloguing-in-Publication Data

A catalogue record for this book is available from the British Library.

ISBN 978-1407-16857-9

Printed and bound by Ashford Colour Press

Due to the nature of the web we cannot guarantee the content or links of any site mentioned. We strongly recommend that teachers check websites before using them in the classroom.

Every effort has been made to trace copyright holders for the works reproduced in this book, and the publishers apologise for any inadvertent omissions.

Extracts from National Curriculum for England, Mathematics Programme of Study
© Crown Copyright. Reproduced under the terms of the Open Government Licence (OGL).
www.nationalarchives.gov.uk/doc/open-government-licence/version/3/

Author Paul Hollin
Editorial Rachel Morgan, Jenny Wilcox, Kim Vernon, Julia Roberts
Artwork Tom Heard at The Bright Agency
Cover and Series Design Neil Salt and Nicolle Thomas
Layout Oxford Designers and Illustrators Ltd

Contents

About the book

This book is part of the Scholastic Booster Classroom Programme. It is designed to be used in conjunction with the Booster Tests Papers and Booster Workbooks.

The introduction provides overview information about how to set up a booster programme and a suggestion of how it could be structured in your school. This book has been written with different units which are numbered for ease-of-reference, but it is designed to work flexibly for your needs and does not need to be covered sequentially (see page 5 for more information). There are also a number of photocopiable resource sheets provided, including an attendance chart, reward certificate and a letter for parents, as well as a curriculum coverage overview to allow you to locate specific needs easily.

Each unit follows the same structure. It is intended each session will take around 20 minutes and each unit could form multiple sessions, if required.

- **Objectives:** the National Curriculum objectives that the session covers are provided.

- **What the children need to know:** a brief summary of the key points that the children need to know about the focus of the session.

- **Test links:** which questions link to this unit from the Booster Test Papers – you can review a previous test the children have taken or work on sample questions collectively.

- **Workbook links:** which pages link to this unit from the Booster Workbook which you can ask children to work on.

- **Support ideas:** a range of different support ideas have been provided for each unit; it is not intended that all of these would be completed in a single session (or that all would need to be completed), rather that you would choose the most appropriate tasks for your children's needs.

- **Review:** provides support for what to look for when reviewing the work children have done to ensure they are comfortable with this area.

- **Beware:** things to be careful of when teaching or common misconceptions that the children might make that you should be aware of.

At the end of the book is a range of summary photocopiable pages. These pages summarise key points from each unit that the children should know along with providing examples. They should be used as an aide-memoire for the children (possibly towards the end of a booster programme as revision and consolidation).

How to set up a booster programme

Each school will devise its own programme of preparation for the Key Stage 1 tests. It is quite possible to prepare children by using whole-class teaching and activities, working through the assessable areas of the curriculum. However, this will not take account of individual needs or the weighting of marks in the papers. Some areas of study are worth far more marks than others and it could be beneficial to spend proportionately more time preparing for these.

Teachers will need to decide how they will support those who need it, while stretching the more able. This could be by targeted teaching within the normal classroom situation or by additional classes. If you are using additional classes outside of school hours, parental permission will be needed; a letter template has been provided for this on page 7.

The following is an example of how to prepare a booster programme using the Booster materials published by Scholastic. In it, the results of each Practice Test are used diagnostically to decide upon areas of the curriculum most in need of reinforcement. It is not sequential and it allows you to plan your own programmes to meet the needs of each child. For example, you may decide that the majority of children are proficient in some areas and need minimal reinforcement, allowing more time to concentrate on individual areas of weakness. Alternatively, you could group children by their areas of weakness and target each one in turn. This could mean that different groups of children are working on different areas of the tests at the same time.

	Teacher	All children	Most children	Some children
10–12 weeks before the test	Introduce the children to the format of the tests. Use Practice Test A. Use the results to identify the areas of weakness of the majority of the children. Share the results with the children. Ensure on-going practice of number skills.	Take Practice Test A.		
8–10 weeks before the test	Use the Booster Programme Teacher's Guide to introduce the children to the areas they have found most difficult.	Teacher-directed work through activities from the Teacher's Guide.	Work individually through some of the questions in the Workbook on the areas they found most difficult.	Work in small groups or individually with support through some of the questions in the Workbook on the areas they found most difficult.

	Teacher	All children	Most children	Some children
6–8 weeks before the test	Review Practice Test A and repeat any problem questions to consolidate knowledge. Use the results to evaluate progress overall. Share the results with the children. Ensure on-going practice of number skills.	Retake Practice Test A problem questions if appropriate.		
4–6 weeks before the test	Work through Booster sessions on areas of the tests that have not been covered so far. Ask the children which areas they feel they need the most support with and include short Booster sessions on those.	Teacher-directed work through the activities from the Teacher's Guide on areas that have not been covered so far in the Booster sessions.	Work individually through some of the questions in the Workbook on the areas they feel they need more support with.	Work in small groups or individually with support through some of the questions in the Workbook on the areas they feel they need more support with.
2–4 weeks before the test	Use Practice Test B. Use the results to evaluate progress overall and specifically in the areas of weakness highlighted in Test B. Share the results with the children. Ensure on-going practice of number skills.	Take Practice Test B.		
1–2 weeks before the test	Prepare and teach short sessions on each of the areas of the test (you may wish to use the summary photocopiable pages at the end of the book). Encourage the children to identify areas of the test they feel they need the most support with. Prepare and teach specific sessions on these areas. Identify areas of weakness for individual children. Assign specific tasks for these areas for each child.	Work through individual activities in the Workbook on all areas of the test, specifically those identified as needing more practice.	Work individually through some of the questions in the Workbook on the areas they feel they need most support with. Complete specific revision activities assigned by the class teacher on areas of weakness.	Work in small groups or individually with support through some of the questions in the Workbook on the areas they found most difficult. Complete specific revision activities assigned by the class teacher on areas of weakness.

Dear Parents and Carers,

As you will be aware, towards the end of Year 2 the children will be sitting their National Curriculum (SATs) tests. This is obligatory for all children attending state schools, and this year will be taking place from _____ to _____. The tests the children will be sitting are:

English: Spelling – around 15 minutes

English: Grammar and Punctuation – around 20 minutes

English: Reading 1 – around 30 minutes

English: Reading 2 – around 40 minutes

Mathematics 1: Arithmetic – around 20 minutes

Mathematics 2: Reasoning – around 35 minutes

The purpose of the tests is to monitor and compare the performance of state schools, but also to check on the abilities and progress of each child. Scores may continue to be used in Key Stage 2 as a benchmark for future performance.

We are planning a series of Booster Classes for children to help them prepare for the tests, which we would like your child to attend, if possible.

Subject: _____

Dates: _____

Day(s): _____

Times: _____

If you are happy for your child to attend, please complete the form below and return it to us.

The best way to support your child though this period is to ensure that they get plenty of sleep and exercise and that they are not unduly worried about the tests. If they do any work at home, try to provide a calm and quiet environment to work in. If you feel the need to do additional work with your child, please speak to us first so that we can work together and avoid duplication or confusion.

If there is anything else you would like us to clarify or provide further information on, do let us know.

With thanks for your support,

The Year 2 team

✂ -

Year 2 Booster Classes

Child's name: _____

I give my permission for my child to attend the Booster Classes after school.

Name: _____ Signed: _____

Objective coverage overview

Session	Objective
1 Understanding numbers	To identify, represent and estimate numbers using different representations, including the number line.
	To recognise the place value of each digit in a 2-digit number (tens, ones).
2 Counting in steps	To count in steps of 2, 3, and 5 from zero, and in 10s from any number, forward and backward.
3 Comparing and ordering numbers	To compare and order numbers from 0 up to 100; use <, > and = signs.
4 Reading and writing numbers	To read and write numbers to at least 100 in numerals and in words.
5 Solving problems with place value and number facts	To use place value and number facts to solve problems.
6 Adding and subtracting	To add and subtract numbers using concrete objects, pictorial representations, and mentally, including: – a 2-digit number and ones – a 2-digit number and tens – two 2-digit numbers – adding three – 1-digit numbers.
7 Using addition and subtraction	To recall and use addition and subtraction facts to 20 fluently, and derive and use related facts up to 100.
	To show that addition of two numbers can be done in any order (commutative) and subtraction of one number from another cannot.
	To recognise and use the inverse relationship between addition and subtraction and use this to check calculations and solve missing number problems.
8 Solving problems with addition and subtraction	To solve problems with addition and subtraction: – using concrete objects and pictorial representations, including those involving numbers, quantities and measures – applying their increasing knowledge of mental and written methods.
9 The 2-, 5- and 10-times tables	To recall and use multiplication and division facts for the 2-, 5- and 10-multiplication tables, including recognising odd and even numbers.
10 Using multiplication and division	To calculate mathematical statements for multiplication and division within the multiplication tables and write them using the multiplication (×), division (÷) and equals (=) signs.
	To show that multiplication of two numbers can be done in any order (commutative) and division of one number by another cannot.
11 Solving problems with multiplication and division	To solve problems involving multiplication and division, using materials, arrays, repeated addition, mental methods and multiplication and division facts, including problems in contexts.
12 Recognising fractions	To recognise, find, name and write fractions $\frac{1}{3}$, $\frac{1}{4}$, $\frac{2}{4}$ and $\frac{3}{4}$ of a length, shape, set of objects or quantity.
13 Using fractions	To write simple fractions for example, $\frac{1}{2}$ of 6 = 3 and recognise the equivalence of $\frac{2}{4}$ and $\frac{1}{2}$.
14 Length and temperature	To choose and use appropriate standard units to estimate and measure length/height in any direction (m/cm) and temperature (°C) to the nearest appropriate unit using thermometers.
15 Mass and capacity	To choose and use appropriate standard units to estimate and measure mass (kg/g) and capacity (l/ml) to the nearest appropriate unit, using scales and measuring vessels.

Session	Objective
16 Comparing measures	To compare and order lengths, mass, volume/capacity and record the results using >, < and =.
17 Money	To recognise and use symbols for pounds (£) and pence (p); combine amounts to make a particular value.
	To find different combinations of coins that equal the same amounts of money.
	To solve simple problems in a practical context involving addition and subtraction of money of the same unit, including giving change.
18 Time	To compare and sequence intervals of time.
	To tell and write the time to 5 minutes, including quarter past/to the hour and draw the hands on a clock face to show these times.
	To know the number of minutes in an hour and the number of hours in a day.
19 2D shapes	To identify and describe the properties of 2D shapes, including the number of sides and line symmetry in a vertical line.
	To compare and sort common 2D shapes and everyday objects.
20 3D shapes	To identify and describe the properties of 3D shapes, including the number of edges, vertices and faces.
	To identify 2D shapes on the surface of 3D shapes (for example, a circle on a cylinder and a triangle on a pyramid).
	To compare and sort common 3D shapes and everyday objects.
21 Patterns and sequences	To order and arrange combinations of mathematical objects in patterns and sequences.
22 Position and direction	To use mathematical vocabulary to describe position, direction and movement, including movement in a straight line and distinguishing between rotation as a turn and in terms of right angles for quarter, half and three-quarter turns (clockwise and anti-clockwise).
23 Tally charts and tables	To interpret and construct tally charts and simple tables.
	To ask and answer simple questions by counting the number of objects in each category and sorting the categories by quantity.
	To ask and answer questions about totalling and comparing categorical data.
24 Block diagrams and pictograms	To interpret and construct simple pictograms and block diagrams.
	To ask and answer simple questions by counting the number of objects in each category and sorting the categories by quantity.
	To ask and answer questions about totalling and comparing categorical data.

Progression chart

Name: _____

Session	Revised	Practised	Achieved
1 Understanding numbers			
2 Counting in steps			
3 Comparing and ordering numbers			
4 Reading and writing numbers			
5 Solving problems with place value and number facts			
6 Adding and subtraction			
7 Using addition and subtraction			
8 Solving problems with addition and subtraction			
9 The 2–, 5– and 10– times tables			
10 Using multiplication and division			
11 Solving problems with multiplication and division			
12 Recognising fractions			
13 Using fractions			
14 Length and temperature			
15 Mass and capacity			
16 Comparing measures			
17 Money			
18 Time			
19 2D shapes			
20 3D shapes			
21 Patterns and sequences			
22 Position and direction			
23 Tally charts and tables			
24 Block diagrams and pictograms			

Attendance chart

Subject: _____

Teacher: _____

Name	1	2	3	4	5	6	7	8	9	10	11	12	13	14	15	16	17	18	19	20	21	22	23	24

Reward certificate

SCHOLASTIC

Well done!

You have completed the Maths Booster Classes.

Name: _____ Date: _____

Your strongest areas are: _____

_____

Areas you might want to practise a bit more are:

_____

1 Understanding numbers

Objectives

- To identify, represent and estimate numbers using different representations, including the number line.
- To recognise the place value of each digit in a 2-digit number (tens, ones).

What the children need to know

- Oral and written representations of numbers up to 100, including digits, objects, number lines and number squares.
- The use of place value in defining 2-digit numbers, moving on to 3-digit numbers.

TEST LINKS
Set A, Paper 2: Q2, 3, 4, 6, 7
Set B, Paper 2: Q1, 2, 3

WORKBOOK LINKS
Pages 6–7

Support ideas

- Provide children with different apparatus (such as Dienes™ equipment, abaci, coloured cubes and so on) to practise making numbers between 1 and 100. Faster thinking can be encouraged by calling out different numbers, displaying them on the whiteboard, or supplying children with sets of cue/flash cards.
- Use a digital abacus on the whiteboard to display random numbers between 1 and 100, limited as appropriate, and have children write down the numeric equivalents. Alternatively, they could shade the numbers in on a 100-square as they appear, or complete a number line if feasible.
- Use a 100-square to examine the patterns of the Base10 system, looking at repeating patterns. Model effective vocabulary by giving each child a square and asking them to move their finger to specific numbers, then moving ten more, ten less, and so on.
- Look at items that are arranged in tens, such as packs of pencils, and consider how these can be counted individually or in their tens (for example, 3 packs of pencils contains 30 pencils).
- It is important for children to have a feel for the magnitude of numbers. Use counters or cubes to practise and develop estimation skills. Check answers through actual counting, grouping counters in piles of ten to aid accuracy and ease.
- Provide small groups of children with two sets of number cards 0–9, and have them make different 2-digit numbers, either as called out by the teacher or by challenging each other to make the amounts, then shading them in on a 100-square.
- Move on to using selective number lines (for example, between 30 and 40), asking children to position numbers on them – initially with dashes to indicate each number in between, then using blank lines to aid estimation skills.

Review

- Children should be able to identify and write numbers from 1 to 100 automatically when hearing them stated orally, and be able to interpret representations using different equipment, such as an abacus.
- They should also be able to find numbers rapidly on number squares and number lines, and insert numbers in the correct spaces.

Beware

- Much of this knowledge can be easily assessed via other mathematics work, though it is worth focusing on it exclusively to check on the security of children's understanding.
- Some equipment work can be very time inefficient, especially when children are counting large numbers of objects. Try to avoid this by using sets of tens, which will also consolidate understanding of place value.

2

Counting in steps

Objectives

- To count in steps of 2, 3, and 5 from zero, and in 10s from any number, forward and backward.

What the children need to know

- How to count on from zero in different steps.
- How to count forwards and backwards in tens from any number.

TEST LINKS
Set A, Paper 2: Q6
Set B, Paper 2: Q8, 15, 19

WORKBOOK LINKS
Pages 8–9

⌄ Support ideas

- Note that although counting equipment may be helpful for those who need additional support, the majority of children are expected to count in an 'abstract' manner, just using numbers on lines, moving on to purely oral work.

- To reinforce step-counting skills, work with both number lines and groups of objects depending on children's needs. Using the children themselves is ideal for counting in twos – two eyes, ears, arms, legs, shoes and so on – which helps to establish the use of numbers to represent any quantity, as well as the number 2 representing pairs. This can also be done for fives and tens (fingers and toes).

- Give the children 100-squares and shade in patterns of 2, 3 and 5, starting with 1–20 initially, and then progressing to 100. Use this to discuss patterns and model both vocabulary and counting skills, providing opportunities for children to consider why the patterns overlap in certain places.

- Ensure that children are very familiar with using a 100-square for counting forwards and backwards in tens. Once they have spotted the pattern, they should be able to do this rapidly, without needing the support of the square.

- Check children's fluency in counting on from 0 to 20 for all the numbers in focus, extending to 30 for 3s and 50 for 5s. This will provide further reinforcement for times-tables facts.

- If appropriate, move on to counting backwards in twos, threes and fives. This will help with children's appreciation of the number system as well as consolidating their knowledge of the number ranges for each of the times tables involved.

- Use number lines with missing numbers and problems in context for groupings of objects, such as grouping children in threes to do particular activities in PE, to develop reasoning skills.

⌄ Review

- Assess children's abilities initially using a 100-square and number lines, progressing to oral counting without support.

- Focus in particular in counting within the range of specific numbers' times-tables ranges (i.e. twos to 20 and so on).

- Consider assessing children's skills in counting in tens as applied to other curriculum areas (for example, 20 more, 10 less).

⌄ Beware

- Some children may start seeing the links to the multiplication tables. This may develop their own competence and speed, but can muddle their peers in group work.

- Children can make the easy mistake of counting from 1 rather than 0, as 100-squares and number lines often do not contain 0.

3

Comparing and ordering numbers

Objectives

To compare and order numbers from 0 up to 100; use <, > and = signs.

What the children need to know

- The magnitude of a number is represented by its digits, read from left to right.
- Numbers can be compared using statements such as is less than, greater than and equals to.

TEST LINKS
Set A, Paper 2: Q7, 12
Set B, Paper 2: Q3

WORKBOOK LINKS
Pages 10–11

⌄ Support ideas

- Spend time looking at pairs of numbers with very different tens and ones digits, such as 17, 18 and 91, 92, and consider with the class how each place value operates, demonstrating that the tens always come first in considering a number's magnitude.
- Likewise, model the use of more than and less than, including the signs > and < for comparing numbers. Provide lots of oral modelling and practice.
- Arrange the children in small groups and give each group a set of flash cards with various 2-digit numbers on them. Challenge the groups to arrange the numbers in ascending and descending order, as well as arranging them to make true statements for comparing any two numbers, using the 'more than' and 'less than' signs.
- Children who need additional support might play snakes and ladders to show increasing to larger numbers, and decreasing to smaller numbers.

⌄ Review

- Children should be able to arrange numbers and use associated vocabulary easily. This should be evident in laying out addition, subtraction and multiplication calculations, where the smaller numbers are usually placed below the larger ones.

⌄ Beware

- Children can easily muddle the meaning of the 'greater than' and 'lesser than' signs. Explaining that the > and < signs are like crocodile mouths usually works, with the wider end at the larger number.

4

Reading and writing numbers

Objectives
- To read and write numbers to at least 100 in numerals and in words.

What the children need to know
- The correct format and spelling for writing numbers in words and digits.

Support ideas

- Spend time reinforcing the need for a hyphen between the words for 2-digit numbers, for example, twenty-one.
- Use flash cards to play memory games – matching pairs of numbers, one in digits, one in words. Encourage as much oral repetition as possible.
- Write random 2-digit numbers on the whiteboard and challenge the class to write them in words.
- Arrange the children in pairs and ask them to challenge each other to write 2-digit numbers in words without seeing the digits of the original.
- For children who need additional practice, play bingo-type games with 100-squares written in words. These may have to be on A3 paper, ideally laminated for re-use.

Review

- Check spellings and hyphen use in writing numbers as words, as well as fluency in reading numbers, both in digits and words.

Beware

- Beware the teens. These are one-off numbers that do not follow the convention of the other numbers up to 100, and need to be learned separately. Ensure children do not confuse saying 'teen' as in 'thirteen' with 'ty' as in 'thirty'. Emphasise the 'n' ending at the end of 'teen'.

TEST LINKS
Set A, Paper 2: Q4
Set B, Paper 2: Q1, 2

WORKBOOK LINKS
Page 12–13

5

Objectives

To use place value and number facts to solve problems.

What the children need to know

How to count on and back in everyday practical contexts.

How to add and subtract numbers using place value and number facts.

Note: addition and subtraction is covered fully in coming units 6–8.)

Solving problems with place value and number facts

TEST LINKS
Set A, Paper 2: Q11, 13, 14, 24
Set B, Paper 2: Q7, 9, 15, 17, 18

WORKBOOK LINKS
Pages 14–15

Support ideas

- Brainstorm with the class things that come in twos, threes, fives and tens, such as eyes, socks, fingers (and thumbs). Model how to calculate numbers by counting on. For example, six boxes of shoes contain 2, 4, 6, 8, 10, 12 shoes altogether.

- Extend the above idea using different scenarios and objects, such as packs of ten pencils, packs of three oranges, and discuss different calculation scenarios, moving on to subtraction – for example, in a shop there are ten packs of three oranges – if three packs are bought how many oranges will remain?

- Progress to problems with remainders, such as four pairs of socks and one odd one; seven packs of ten pencils and three spares; three packs of five chocolate bars with two single bars, and so on.

- Model and practise using partitioning to support subtraction, such as $23 = 13 + 10$.

- Provide a range of problems that require children to focus on the value of each digit in 2-digit numbers to solve them (see Workbook for examples).

Review

- Note which children are proficient in counting in steps of 2, 3, 5 and 10.

- Via discussion and oral answering, note children who are not secure in their awareness of the place value of digits in determining number names and sizes.

- Look for children who are struggling to apply skills and facts to problems, particularly where the problems are in word or picture form – consider whether children are able to apply their mathematics knowledge effectively.

- Observe whether children can partition 2-digit numbers confidently, in particular applying this skill to some subtractions. (This should be borne in mind when revising addition and subtraction skills.)

Beware

- Remember that some children may automatically use number bonds or multiplication facts to answer questions and solve problems – do not interrupt this unless it is causing children to answer questions incorrectly/inappropriately, but encourage them to use counting on as a way of double-checking their work (and indeed the reverse can be applied for those who seem confident and secure enough).

6

Adding and subtracting

Objectives

- To add and subtract numbers using concrete objects, pictorial representations, and mentally, including:
  - › a 2-digit number and ones
  - › a 2-digit number and tens
  - › two 2-digit numbers
  - › adding three 1-digit numbers.

What the children need to know

- Methods for adding and subtracting using objects, pictures, number lines and mental methods.
- Number bonds to 20 and their use for deriving other facts, including subtraction facts and calculations beyond 20.

TEST LINKS
Set A, Paper 1: Q1–8, 11–13, 16, 17, 22
Set A, Paper 2: Q21
Set B, Paper 1: Q1–7, 10–12, 18, 20, 23–25

WORKBOOK LINKS
Pages 16–17

⌄ Support ideas

- Following on from children's work with counting in steps, provide them with apparatus that allows both counting in tens and in ones, such as Dienes™ equipment and abaci. Use short, regular sessions to practise both making 2-digit numbers and performing rapid addition and subtraction using the apparatus, selecting 1- or 2-digit numbers as appropriate.
- A useful transition to using pictorial representations can be provided by using drawings of Dienes™ and abaci (or asking children to do their own) on to which they draw and delete to calculate given amounts.
- Whatever the ability range across the class, continue to provide short regular sessions aimed at fluency with number bonds to 20, introducing the addition of three one-digit numbers, using the preferred mental methods as per the school's mathematics policy.
- Use number lines to show calculations too, using partitioning as appropriate.
- If appropriate, introduce the use of inverse calculations to check answers – depending on ability levels this should be introduced with care.
- Arrange the children in groups and provide each with two sets of flash cards – one of two-digit numbers and the other of one-digit numbers. Challenge them to shuffle and randomly turn over one card in each pile, and to write the answer to the mental addition and subtraction these numbers generate. (This can be simplified to just adding and subtracting tens or ones as desired).
- Use regular, short, quick-fire Q&A sessions to practise mental calculations within desired number ranges. Use these sessions to model good practice and correct vocabulary as much as possible.

⌄ Review

- First and foremost, look for children who are not secure in their basic understanding of place value, especially when adding a one-digit number that requires the tens value to be increased.
- Note if children are competent in both pictorial and mental methods for the addition and subtraction skills presented. Try to discuss their answers with them and note how clearly they explain their work.

⌄ Beware

- In completing the workbook children may use other skills that are presented in subsequent units. If this is a sign of competence then all well and good, but do check that they are secure with number bonds and related facts.

7 Using addition and subtraction

Objectives

To recall and use addition and subtraction facts to 20 fluently, and derive and use related facts up to 100.

To show that addition of two numbers can be done in any order (commutative) and subtraction of one number from another cannot.

To recognise and use the inverse relationship between addition and subtraction.

What the children need to know

Fluent number bonds to 20.

How to use partitioning for adding and subtracting.

There is commutativity in addition, and not in subtraction.

How to use inverse relationships to check calculations.

TEST LINKS

Set A, Paper 1: Q1–8, 11–13, 16, 17, 22

Set A, Paper 2: Q14, 18, 21

Set B, Paper 1: Q1–7, 10–12, 18, 20, 23–25

Set B, Paper 2: Q11

WORKBOOK LINKS

Pages 18–19

Support ideas

- Provide regular short sessions for the class to practise their number bonds to 20 – using rapid-fire Q&A as well as peer-to-peer questioning.

- Using methods outlined in previous Unit 5, practise using number bonds to find related addition and subtraction facts to 100. As appropriate, look at partitioning as a mental method.

- Provide each child with a 100-square, and challenge them to use it to practise adding and subtracting 2-digit numbers mentally, ensuring that they only work with numbers they are comfortable with. Ask the class to write down each calculation once they have solved it mentally, to help increase awareness of current abilities and next steps. Use the terms 'sum' and 'difference' as appropriate.

- Using the previous suggestion (using a 100-square to practise mental calculations), ask the children to rewrite each calculation with their two chosen numbers reversed, and to investigate the outcome. Children will quickly see the basic law of commutative behaviour in addition, but not subtraction (some children may also know this for multiplication from their times tables' work).

- As above, encourage the children to use inverse calculations to check all of their calculations. This skill can be enhanced through other activities – quick-fire questioning and flash cards for random calculations – where a calculation is chosen, and rather than being answered the inverse calculation is immediately stated, (noting that there are always two possible inverse calculations for verifying an addition).

Review

- Note which children are secure and fluent in their number bonds to 20, and which are also confident in using these bonds to derive related facts to 100.

- Use one-to-one conversations to determine individual understanding of commutativity in addition, and also for assessing understanding of inverse calculations for checking work.

Beware

- Although the workbook and the activities suggested above are aimed at revision, children who are not ready for it may be confused by work aimed at investigating the commutative law, as well as inverse calculations for checking work. These activities should only be presented when children are secure enough to understand them.

8

Objectives

- To solve problems with addition and subtraction:
  - using concrete objects and pictorial representations, including those involving numbers, quantities and measures
  - applying their increasing knowledge of mental and written methods.

What the children need to know

- Addition and subtraction can be used to solve real-life problems.
- All methods and skills can be used as appropriate.
- Presenting work neatly and logically is important.

TEST LINKS

Set A, Paper 2: Q11, 13, 14, 24

Set B, Paper 2: Q7, 9, 17, 18

WORKBOOK LINKS

Pages 20–22

Solving problems with addition and subtraction (extended un

⊗ Support ideas

- Teachers should model and encourage oral discussion and explanation of ho to solve problems and how to decide which mathematical operations should be used. Talking can help clarify and consolidate thinking, and supports those children who need it.
- Display a set of objects or images on the whiteboard and use these for rapid practice of number bonds in context. For example, *There are nine pencils – hov many will remain if I take four away?* Use this approach to vary thinking and problem solving, for example, *There are nine pencils here, after ten minutes there are only three – how many have been removed?* Note how vocabulary can incluc specific mathematical terms (*subtract*) or more everyday terms (*removed*).
- Provide a range of resources and encourage children to create their own problems. They can write these themselves or have an adult scribe for them Note that money problems are covered later in Unit 17, so for the present focus on problems that do not involve money.
- Moving on to problems with larger numbers, children will need practice in using preferred methods for adding and subtracting such numbers, using partitioning and/or number lines and so on. Continue to work on this using discussion and visualisation, encouraging answer-checking at all times: use both quick methods – *Does it feel about right? Does it make sense?* – to more thorough checking using inverse calculations.

⊗ Review

- Look for children who are providing correct solutions but with workings that don't make apparent sense – check whether they truly understand the concepts or have developed their own strategies for solving problems.
- Check presentation of workings, which is significant for the second test paper at Key Stage 1, and look also for evidence that children are considering, and ideally checking, their answers.

⊗ Beware

- Remember that the actual test paper will also involve problems that use multiplication and division, and problems that combine other curriculum areas with addition and subtraction, such as data handling. Different teachers will prefer different approaches to focusing on such problems.

9

The 2-, 5- and 10-times tables

Objectives

To recall and use multiplication and division facts for the 2-, 5- and 10-multiplication tables, including recognising odd and even numbers.

What the children need to know

How to use a multiplication square for finding and checking multiplication and division facts.

Every multiplication fact provides four different facts – two multiplication and two division facts.

The 2-, 5- and 10-times tables have several facts in common.

How to represent multiplication and division calculations in writing using the × and ÷ signs.

How to recognise and know odd and even numbers.

TEST LINKS
Set A, Paper 1: Q14, 15, 18, 21, 23, 25
Set A, Paper 2: Q3
Set B, Paper 1: Q8, 9, 13, 14, 17, 21, 22

WORKBOOK LINKS
Pages 23–25

Support ideas

- Use regular short sessions to develop fluency with the multiplication square. Use a large poster or a digital version to model and discuss rapid finding of any facts from the 2-, 5- and 10-times tables.

- Use both a multiplication square and equipment to consolidate children's understanding of the relationship between multiplication and division, noting calculations in sets (for example, $2 \times 3 = 6$, $3 \times 2 = 6$, $6 \div 2 = 3$, $6 \div 3 = 2$). This can be extended to a call and answer activity, whereby the teacher calls out a known fact, such as *Five times two equals ten*, and the children have to respond with a related fact, such as *Ten divided by two equals five*.

- Link 10-times tables work to children's place value knowledge, and 5-times tables work to clock faces (see Unit 18).

- Demonstrate and practise the representation of multiplication as arrays, such as two rows of three dots gives six dots. Representing calculations in this way can help children to visualise the processes, and is a useful skill in its own right for trickier problems that use different multiplication tables.

- Present and display odd and even numbers from 1 to 10, and discuss the definition of each. Demonstrate how these rules can be used to easily spot whether any number is odd or even, noting in particular numbers that end in zero as being even.

- Ask the children to investigate the 2-, 5- and 10-times tables on a multiplication square, looking for patterns in overlapping tables (for example, $2 \times 5 = 1 \times 10$) and challenging them to try to explain these occurrences. In addition, ask them to look at the occurrence of odd and even numbers in each of these tables, and to consider whether there are any rules they can spot as to whether the product of two numbers will be even or odd (odd × odd = odd, the other three permutations provide an even answer).

Review

- Straightforward arithmetic questions will easily reveal how secure children's understanding of these tables is. Although the arithmetic paper just requires answers, children should feel confident in using preferred methods for finding and checking their answers.

- In problem-solving work, check that number facts are being used securely alongside other thinking to solve problems correctly.

Beware

- Reciting tables in order does not guarantee proficiency or understanding. Mix up as many forms of practice as possible.

- Most of the support ideas above should be done in short bursts alongside other mathematical work – a bit like not studying vocabulary in isolation when introducing a new language to children.

10 Using multiplication and division

Objectives

- To calculate mathematical statements for multiplication and division within the multiplication tables and write them using the multiplication (×), division (÷) and equals (=) signs.
- To show that multiplication of two numbers can be done in any order (commutative) and division of one number by another cannot.

What the children need to know

- Fluent recall of 2-, 5- and 10-times tables.and related facts for division.
- How to use arrays.
- How to recognise and demonstrate commutativity in multiplication, and not in division.
- How to use inverse relationships.

Support ideas

- Continue using the support ideas from the previous unit to provide short, quick sessions on reciting and recalling different aspects of these times tables.
- Develop awareness of the relationship between multiplication and division, providing sets of cards with numbers on relating to specific facts, and have children re-arrange them to produce related facts. Use short, regular sessions to instil the idea that every fact has three related facts.
- It may be desirable to relate repeated addition to arrays, or at least get children into the habit of looking at a repeated addition and restating it as a multiplication, using vocabulary such as 'lots of' and 'times', and where appropriate progressing to the shortest form of statement (for example, *Four threes are twelve*).
- Provide children with sets of cubes, counters or beads, and have them challenge each other by making arrays and asking their peers to make mathematical statements for them. In particular, it is interesting to adjust arrays, where one child might make a 5 by 2 array, which would be identified as 5 × 2 = 10, and then for another child to add a row, making 6 × 2, and so on.
- Commutativity can be difficult for children to understand. At this stage, it may be best to just provide practice in investigating it through multiplication, perhaps using arrays to show connecting multiplication facts. Division-wise, the non-commutative nature of this operation often needs practical examples to enlighten children – the difficulty is that the divisions are often beyond their knowledge and experience, and they may have to take their confusion as proof of the non-commutative nature. Providing examples for children in a measured, modelled manner will be beneficial.

Review

- Look for mastery of both the times tables themselves (for 2, 5 and 10) as well as competent understanding of the related facts (these will be used for solving problems in Unit 11).
- Children should talk about and use arrays and repeated addition in a competent manner.

Beware

- Commutativity can be confusing to children with insecure skills and knowledge – use it lightly.

11

Solving problems with multiplication and division (extended unit)

Objectives

To solve problems involving multiplication and division, using materials, arrays, repeated addition, mental methods and multiplication and division facts, including problems in contexts.

What the children need to know

Multiplication and division can be used to solve real-life problems.

All methods and skills can be used as appropriate.

Presenting work neatly and logically is important.

Work can be checked using inverse calculations.

TEST LINKS

Set A, Paper 1: Q14, 15, 18, 21, 23, 25

Set A, Paper 2: Q11, 20, 25

Set B, Paper 1: Q8, 9, 13, 14, 17, 21, 22

Set B, Paper 2: Q15, 20, 21, 23

WORKBOOK LINKS

Pages 29–32

Support ideas

- Teachers should model and encourage oral discussion and explanation of how to solve problems and how to decide which mathematical operations should be used – talking is vital to clarify and consolidate understanding.

- Display a set of objects or images on the whiteboard and use these for rapid practice of multiplication facts in context. For example, *If there are five books on every table, and there are three tables, how many books are there?* Use this approach to vary thinking and problem solving, such as: *In another room there are 40 books. If there are five books on each table, how many tables are there?*

- For all problems, work them through with the class and discuss the mathematical approach used and model the clear presentation of written work.

- Provide children with a range of resources and encourage them to create their own problems. They can write these themselves or have an adult scribe for them. Note that money problems are covered later in Unit 18, for the present focus on problems that do not involve money.

- Provide practice in using preferred methods for multiplying and dividing, encouraging answer-checking at all times, both quick – *Does it feel about right? Does it make sense?* – to more thorough checking using inverse calculations.

- Simple multi-step problems should also be introduced, such as six packs of ten pencils with three pencils given away – how many remain? Visualising the problem, drawing it, thinking through the logical steps, presenting workings, should all be modelled and discussed.

Review

- Look for children who are providing correct solutions but with workings that don't make apparent sense – check whether they truly understand the concepts or have developed their own strategies for solving problems.

- Check presentation of workings, which is significant for the second test paper at Key Stage 1, and look also for evidence that children are evaluating and checking their answers.

Beware

- Although the arithmetic paper will likely have more marks for multiplication and division than the reasoning paper, the best way to consolidate children's understanding of these skills is by applying them in problem-based contexts.

12 Recognising fractions

Objectives

- To recognise, find, name and write fractions $\frac{1}{3}$, $\frac{1}{4}$, $\frac{2}{4}$ and $\frac{3}{4}$ of a length, shape, set of objects or quantity.

What the children need to know

- How to recognise, name and write simple fractions.
- How to determine the fraction of lengths and shapes.
- How to determine the fraction of sets of objects or quantities.

TEST LINKS
Set A, Paper 2: Q15, 19, 20
Set B, Paper 2: Q6, 13,

WORKBOOK LINKS
Pages 33–34

Support ideas

- Create a permanent display of the fractions children need to know, showing them in their numeric form, in words and with visual representations – dots, segment of a circle, part of a line and so on.
- Create sets of flash cards with the different numeric, word and pictorial representations of the key fractions. Use these for rapid recognition activities, as well as matching and memory games.
- Move on to showing each fraction as a proportion of different shapes or sets of objects, to help consolidate understanding of the concept of what fractions are.
- Arrange children in pairs or small groups and have them challenge each other to define fractions. This can be supported either with sets of shapes, such as quarter-circles, small plastic squares, or photocopied sheets of blank circles. Children should create a fraction and challenge their peers to identify it.
- The above activity can be used to extend children's thinking. Can they make statements about the number of fractions that make up a whole (for example, *Three thirds make a whole*)? Can they make comparative statements about different fractions (for example, *One third is more than one quarter*). Although this is beyond the scope of the Key Stage 1 curriculum, it is valid for consolidation of their understanding.
- Try presenting children with a number line, 0–1, and work with them to arrange key fractions on this line. This can lead to counting in fractions beyond 1 and up to 10.
- Using pre-prepared images of groups of objects, display these on the whiteboard and work with the class to calculate different fractional amounts of each quantity. (If you wish to find both thirds and quarters of an amount, the total number of objects must of course be divisible by three and four).
- You can challenge the thinking of more confident children by having them draw a range of different line lengths, and asking them to find fractional lengths of each (for example, $\frac{1}{4}$ *of 20cm = 5cm*). This leads on to Unit 13 where fractions of numbers are calculated.

Review

- Check that children understand the fundamental concept of fractions, moving on to correct written representations and application to dividing groups of objects, shapes and lines.

Beware

- In problems where a fraction of a quantity of an object or group is removed (for example, *He ate one piece of pizza. How much did he eat?*), the visual representation of the remaining amount can be confusing. Encourage children to use their hands to cover shapes, or use a pencil to draw/encircle the amount to be focused on.

Using fractions

Objectives

To write simple fractions for example, $\frac{1}{2}$ of 6 = 3 and recognise the equivalence of $\frac{2}{4}$ and $\frac{1}{2}$.

What the children need to know

Fractions of numbers can be written as mathematical statements using the word 'of'.

The calculations relate to division facts from the times tables.

Support ideas

Note: Finding $\frac{1}{4}$, $\frac{1}{3}$ and $\frac{1}{2}$ of quantities should be presented initially, with $\frac{3}{4}$ being presented as a 'special case' (see last idea in this list).

- Although the range of objectives for using fractions at this age is quite small, it is possible to use this unit to consolidate children's mathematical thinking, helping them to see the links that fractions have with multiplication and division.

- Bearing in mind the activities in the previous unit, identifying fractions of groups of objects, repeat these activities (for example, circling three out of six dots to identify one half), and then write the mathematical sentence underneath (i.e. $\frac{1}{2}$ of 6 = 3), using the opportunity to model both the written and verbal form of the statement.

- Use flash cards for $\frac{1}{2}$, $\frac{1}{3}$ and $\frac{1}{4}$ alongside appropriate flash cards of whole numbers to generate random calculations for short practice sessions. Teachers may wish to include whole numbers that do not lend themselves to calculation, such as 5, to help reinforce the concept of whole division.

- Demonstrate the meaning of 'of' in fraction statements, showing that it is the same as a multiplication sign. When appropriate, move on to the use of divide in these calculations, linking them to times tables facts.

- The fraction $\frac{3}{4}$ singularly introduces the use of a numerator greater than one. Be sure to spend additional time looking at visual representations for three quarters, and modelling how to identify three quarters of a group of objects. Demonstrate that if one quarter of the amount is a certain number, then each of the three quarters will contain this amount. This is introducing the concept of multiplying by the numerator. Also, if desired, point out that if one quarter of a group of objects or a number is a certain amount, then three quarters must be the remainder, as one quarter and three quarters make a whole (this is introducing the concept of adding and subtracting fractions).

Review

- Look for children who are using strategies (such as drawing dots or circles) to complete these calculations compared to those who are using mental calculations, or indeed answering 'automatically'. For the latter, try posing questions using larger numbers (for example, $\frac{1}{2}$ of 32).

- Ensure that children are showing working correctly where necessary.

Beware

- Some children will find the transition to numbers-only representations difficult. Provide them with lots of aural practice in treating the work as statements rather than calculations, using continued visual representations or apparatus as necessary.

TEST LINKS
Set A, Paper 1: Q9, 10, 19, 20, 24
Set B, Paper 1: Q15, 16, 19

WORKBOOK LINKS
Pages 35–37

14 Length and temperature

Objectives

- To choose and use appropriate standard units to estimate and measure length/height in any direction (m/cm) and temperature (°C) to the nearest appropriate unit using thermometers.

What the children need to know

- How to correctly use, read and interpret a ruler to measure lengths in cm or m.
- How to correctly use, read and interpret a thermometer to measure temperature in °C.
- How to write lengths and temperatures using the correct units.
- How to estimate lengths and temperatures based on an understanding of the size of a standard unit.

TEST LINKS
Set B, Paper 2: Q10, 13, 14

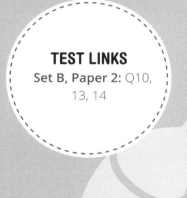

WORKBOOK LINKS
Pages 38–40

Support ideas

- The obviously practical nature of these curriculum areas is harder to assess in paper-based tests, although drawing and measuring length questions should be expected. As such, although it may be wise to provide children with further practical experience to strengthen their knowledge, test preparation is probably best focused around tackling paper-based challenges.
- Review and model correct use of a ruler (digital versions are useful for clear demonstration), checking that children understand the placement of zero and the reading of scales. If a digital version is available, use quick-fire Q&A sessions to estimate and then measure a range of straight lines.
- Provide ample practice of drawing and measuring straight lines with suitable cm-scaled rulers, moving on to measuring the lengths of different images – ideally using ones created specifically for the task (at this age, measurements to the nearest mm are not expected).
- Measurements in metres are trickier to provide experience and practice in, but with the basics understood and children well-practised in measuring cm, it is possible to provide practice in test-type questions. It is more likely that questions involving metres will be used in comparing measures. This is tackled a little in this unit, and more so in the next one. Nevertheless, any examples and modelling of measuring using a metre ruler is advisable, as well as providing a basic reinforcement of the relationship of cm to m.
- Moving on to temperature, the above ideas can also be used with a digital thermometer, providing revision for both thermometer use as well as the Celsius temperature scale.
- For both length and temperature, provide plenty opportunities for estimation before measuring and checking quantities, which helps to consolidate understanding of the units and quantities involved, and stress the importance of writing units (cm, m or °C) correctly after the actual measurement.

Review

- Check that children are able to use a ruler correctly, both for creating and measuring straight lines. For measuring pictures, ensure that they have a suitable procedure for identifying and aligning the appropriate two points to define length.
- Ensure that children can both read and write temperatures using the °C units correctly.

Beware

- Rulers incorporating mm scales between cm markings can be confusing. Be sure to show children, and practise, how to read only the cm markings.
- Similarly, avoid using thermometers with Fahrenheit markings on them.

15 Mass and capacity

Objectives

- To choose and use appropriate standard units to estimate and measure mass (kg/g) and capacity (l/ml) to the nearest appropriate unit, using scales and measuring vessels.

What the children need to know

- How to correctly use, read and interpret scales to measure mass in g or kg.
- How to correctly use, read and interpret measuring containers to measure capacity in ml or l.
- How to write mass and capacity using the correct units.
- How to estimate masses and capacities based on an understanding of the size of a standard unit.

TEST LINKS
Set A, Paper 2: Q16

WORKBOOK LINKS
Pages 41–42

⊙ Support ideas

- As with length and temperature, the practical nature of these curriculum areas is harder to assess in paper-based tests. As such, although it may be wise to provide children with further practical experience to strengthen their knowledge, test preparation is probably best focused around tackling paper-based challenges.
- Use real or digital measuring equipment to provide practice in taking readings. In particular, focus on how readings increase as more mass/fluid is added. This can be developed by playing *Guess the mass* games, where children have to guess the mass of, for example, a bag of marbles. Once guesses are made, useful thinking and reinforcement can be achieved by weighing the marbles incrementally – adding a few at a time (ideally to a digital scale) and noting how the reading gradually increases, and further prediction work can ensue as each marble is added.
- Adopt a similar approach to estimating and measuring capacity – both in filling and emptying vessels.
- Create sets of flash cards showing images of items, as well as separate cards showing their mass written in numerals, and showing grams or kilograms, as well as a separate set of images and capacities in millilitres and litres. Use the flash cards for rapid estimation and oral practice, as well as the usual matching and memory games.
- Throughout all activities, model and reinforce the use of the full words and their abbreviations – for example, millilitres and ml.

⊙ Review

- Check whether children have a clear sense of a millilitre versus a litre, and a gram versus a kilogram, and can use this to provide reasonable estimates, and to accurately match an object to its given mass.
- Check that they are able to read equipment correctly.

⊙ Beware

- Teachers may prefer to revise and review mass and capacity separately – presenting them together can muddle rather than clarify their differences for some children.
- The main issue with images is that they are often not to the same scale – an image of a car might be smaller than the image of a pencil. This can confuse some children.

16

Comparing measures

Objectives

- To compare and order lengths, mass, volume/capacity and record the results using >, < and =.

What the children need to know

- Objects can have more than one quality that can be measured: a mass, a capacity and/or dimensions of length. For any object, these qualities can be compared and objects can be arranged according to the relative sizes of these quantities.
- We can only compare like with like: mass with mass, length with length, and capacity with capacity.
- We can use language and signs for comparing quantities.

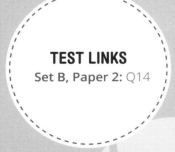

TEST LINKS
Set B, Paper 2: Q14

WORKBOOK LINKS
Pages 43–45

Support ideas

- It is important for children to use terminology in context. Try to use as much discussion as possible when looking at and comparing measures.
- Mix up length, mass and capacity. It is important to identify the measure that is to be used as well as comparing it.
- If possible, bring a range of small objects and containers to the classroom, and ask the children to work in groups to measure the length (and height/width if appropriate), mass and capacity for each one. Create a chart that can either be displayed for all to see, or used on the interactive whiteboard. Once the data on the chart has been verified, return to it regularly to ask questions and make statements. For example, the conker's mass is half the tennis ball's mass; the mug has twice the capacity of the cup; the toy car is the same length as the box; the mass of the tin is greater than that of the cup's; the width of the box is less than that of the tin, and so on. (Notice how the different measures are being considered for the same objects).
- Provide lots of modelling of the correct use of <, > and =. Children easily confuse the first two – one way of remembering is that it is a greedy crocodile's mouth, and the bigger quantity always goes at the wide end.
- To provide focused practice for any one measure, provide sets of picture cards with weight, capacity or length written on them. Have the children work alone or in groups to arrange these in ascending and descending order, as well as challenging them to make statements. For example, they might turn over two cards at random, and make a 'greater than', 'less than', 'twice as', 'half as' or even 'equals' statement about the two quantities shown.
- Note also that ordering and comparing measures is good reinforcement for place value work in general – emphasising the links with different curriculum areas is usually a good thing, especially when oral discussion and practice is used for rapid reinforcement.

Review

- Check that children are using the greater than (>) and less than (<) signs the right way round.
- Check that children are confident in comparing like with like quantities.

Beware

- Grams and millilitres are hard to compare against kilograms and litres at this age, as children's presumed knowledge of numbers is only to 100. Avoid crossing over between sub-units.

17

Money (extended unit)

Objectives

- To recognise and use symbols for pounds (£) and pence (p); combine amounts to make a particular value.
- To find different combinations of coins that equal the same amounts of money.
- To solve simple problems in a practical context involving addition and subtraction of money of the same unit, including giving change.

What the children need to know

- Different coins have different values.
- Different combinations of coins can be used to make the same value.
- Money is shown in writing using the '£' and 'p' symbols.
- Monetary amounts can be added and subtracted.

TEST LINKS
Set A, Paper 2: Q5
Set B, Paper 2: Q5, 17, 25

WORKBOOK LINKS
Pages 46–48

Support ideas

- Use images of coins on the interactive whiteboard to demonstrate equivalences – ten 1p coins have the same value as one 10p coin and so on.
- Spend time looking at gradually increasing amounts and work with the class to consider how each one can be made using combinations of coins. It is important that children appreciate that they are not limited to one of each coin type (images of coins are often presented like this and can be confusing).
- Move on to display particular amounts and work with the class to consider combinations of coins that can make that amount. Spend time on this – it is important for children to appreciate that different sets of coins have the same value.
- Provide children with plastic coins so that they can practise making different amounts (the coins obviously act as a counting aid, which is very helpful to any children struggling with this work). Move on to presenting different amounts for children to make but without coins to handle (if necessary display an image of one of each coin on the whiteboard or on a display).
- Use practical scenarios, using small amounts, to introduce or review the concept of giving change. This differs from totalling amounts with coins in that it is usually just the difference between amount and coin(s) tendered that needs to be evaluated. Move on to providing questions (as in the workbook) that present problems in written form.

Review

- Ensure that children are fluent in recognising and counting coins, and can write monetary amounts correctly using the '£' and 'p' symbols.
- Check children's ability to make an amount using different coins. This will obviously link to their general numeracy abilities, though some children may well find working with coins easier than abstract numbers.
- If any children are struggling with the problem-solving aspect of money, consider where the difficulty lies – is it coin recognition, arithmetic skills, or general comprehension?

Beware

- Some children will struggle without visual images of coins. There is nothing to stop them, time permitting, from drawing these coins on test papers to help them visualise the problem.
- Occasionally money problems might involve two-steps. Encourage children to approach these with 'common sense', clearly stating the order of the calculations.

18

Time (extended unit)

Objectives

- To compare and sequence intervals of time.
- To tell and write the time to 5 minutes, including quarter past/to the hour and draw the hands on a clock face to show these times.
- To know the number of minutes in an hour and the number of hours in a day.

What the children need to know

- There are 60 minutes in an hour and 24 hours in a day.
- An analogue clock is divided into 12 5-minute intervals, with specific rules for reading it correctly.
- The long hand tells us minutes, the short hand tells us hours.
- Intervals of time can be ordered just like any other measure.

TEST LINKS
Set A, Paper 2: Q9
Set B, Paper 2: Q22

WORKBOOK LINKS
Pages 49–51

Support ideas

- Focus on the role of the minute hand. Use a virtual or display-based guide to telling the time. Ideally this should include removable/hide-able labels for each digit showing five-past, ten-past, and so on. This can be used regularly to facilitate quick-fire questions and quizzes. Initially, practise saying each time in sequence (i.e. starting with five past and moving around the clock), progressing to random times), modelling good vocabulary as you go.
- Extend the above activity by removing the hands from the clock and calling out times, challenging the class to agree on where the hands should go.
- Focus on the role of the hour hand. Show a clock face with only the minute-hand showing, set at for example, twenty past. Call out different hours to gradually build children's understanding of the relative position of the hour hand, showing how this is positioned exactly halfway between two numbers when it is half-past the hour.
- Play desk-based *What's the time Mr Wolf?*: Gather the children and decide on an hourly time that you want to practise (for example, hours, half-past, quarter-past or quarter-to). Move the clock hands at several times their normal speed. When the focus time appears, the children have to call out *What's the time Mr Wolf?*, and then answer also.
- Play *Bing, bang, bong*. Similar to the above activity, except focusing on the minute hand. Select three times that you want to practise with the class (for example, twenty past, quarter-to and o'clock). Start moving the hands around, and challenge the children to shout bing, bang or bong as appropriate when any one time is reached. They then tell the actual time, paying heed to the hour-hand too.
- Display pairs of clocks and discuss the time interval between them, moving on to setting one time then asking children to set a time on the second clock at a later interval, starting with simple one-hour intervals and then progressing to fractions of an hour.

Review

- Check that children can read clocks correctly and use sensible strategies for finding intervals between times.
- Ensure that children can read and write written times, as well as draw times correctly on clock faces.

Beware

- The most common difficulty in reading analogue clocks is the role of the hour hand, and how to interpret it when it is between numbers. Some of the activities above help to address this.

19

2D shapes

Objectives

- To identify and describe the properties of 2D shapes, including the number of sides and line symmetry in a vertical line.
- To compare and sort common 2D shapes and everyday objects.

What the children need to know

- How to recognise, name and know the different quadrilaterals and polygons.
- How to compare and sort shapes according to their properties using precise vocabulary.
- How to recognise and identify vertical line symmetry.
- How to read and write the names of the shapes appropriate to word reading and spelling.
- Draw lines and shapes using a straight edge.

TEST LINKS
Set A, Paper 2: Q1, 10

WORKBOOK LINKS
Pages 52–53

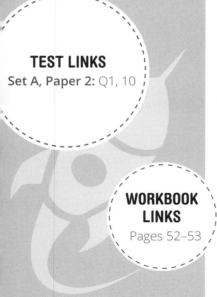

⊙ Support ideas

- Use a slideshow of different 2D shapes and their names – on separate slides – to randomly practise recognition with short, quick-fire quizzes. This can be done as separate activities for both polygons and the quadrilaterals. Use the activity to model and reinforce the generic vocabulary for the features of the shapes – 'sides', 'vertices' and 'angles'.
- Create sets of cards showing both the 2D shapes and their names separately, and challenge the children to play memory activities – *Kim's game* and *Pelmanism* – as well as using the cards to play descriptive games, where they must describe features without naming a shape and their partner must deduce it. This can also extend to drawing activities – draw what is described, guess what someone is drawing, spelling practice and so on.
- Create a selection of sorting charts on large sheets of paper, with a variety of headings, such as 'Shapes with even numbers of sides/odd numbers'. Use these to practise drawing and spelling of shapes.
- If possible, use software or construct a slideshow to show how mirror symmetry works for shapes – ideally introducing a vertical line of symmetry and showing how the shape 'flips' onto itself.
- Use plastic or wooden shapes to draw around and then cut out to investigate the symmetry of each shape. It is equally important to look at non-symmetrical shapes, and to remember that at this age only vertical symmetry will be requested in the national tests.

⊙ Review

- Ensure that children are secure in identifying and naming common polygons and quadrilaterals, as well as reading and spelling all the names.
- Check the accuracy of both identifying and drawing lines of symmetry.
- Note whether children are competent in sorting shapes according to different criteria – considering children's sorting skills and their knowledge of shapes separately – the two skills, while not exclusive, have their own particular facets and tricky areas.

⊙ Beware

- Remember, the plural of 'vertex' is irregular – 'vertices'.
- Some children may have an understanding of symmetry beyond vertical, but they need to be aware that only vertical symmetry will be covered in the national tests.
- Activities that practise sorting skills may not necessarily reveal weaknesses in shape knowledge if children's understanding of sorting skills is insecure.

20

3D shapes

Objectives

- To identify and describe the properties of 3D shapes, including the number of edges, vertices and faces.
- To identify 2D shapes on the surface of 3D shapes (for example, a circle on a cylinder and a triangle on a pyramid).
- To compare and sort common 3D shapes and everyday objects.

What the children need to know

- Recognise, name and know the different 3D shapes.
- Compare and sort 3D shapes according to their properties using precise vocabulary.
- Recognise and name 2D shapes that form faces on 3D shapes.
- Read and write the names of the shapes appropriate to word reading and spelling.

TEST LINKS
Set A, Paper 2: Q23
Set B, Paper 2: Q4

WORKBOOK LINKS
Pages 54–55

Support ideas

- Provide as much tactile experience as possible, ideally using sets of wooden or plastic shapes. Encourage oral discussion around shapes to consolidate vocabulary.
- If possible and/or appropriate, use sticky labels on shapes to name shapes, name faces, identify features, number faces, and so on.
- If available, use digital versions of 3D shapes and rotate and examine them on the whiteboard, using them for quick-fire questions around shapes' names and properties.
- Practise sorting skills using charts on large sheets of paper, with a variety of headings, such as 'shapes with square faces/shapes without a square face', 'shapes with six faces/shapes without six faces'). This can be made much more difficult by removing the actual shapes and limiting it to memory.
- Use modelling clay and/or maths construction equipment to build 3D shapes. Discuss both how shapes can be changed (for example, how to make a cuboid bigger) and the limitations of construction kits (for example, try to build a cylinder or cone) and the difficulty of using clay to make accurate shapes.
- Play the *What am I?* game, where children explain features of a chosen shape one-by-one and challenge their peers to identify it. Lists of shapes' properties can either be written in advance or, if appropriate, the children might generate their own lists – this can be extended by challenging children to write more complex statements (for example, *I do not have a square face*).
- Use spare minutes to practise spellings (including properties – 'face', 'edge', 'vertex', and common 2D face names – 'square', 'rectangle', 'circle'), as well as matching 3D shape names to definitions.

Review

- Ensure that children are secure in naming the features of 3D shapes (faces, edges, vertices).
- Check that children are secure in both reading and spelling the names of 3D shapes.
- Pay particular attention to activities that practise sorting skills – these will not necessarily reveal weaknesses in shape knowledge if children's understanding of sorting skills is insecure.

Beware

- Teachers may find it preferable to review 3D work on separate occasions to 2D shapes to avoid muddling children.
- Remember, the plural of 'vertex' is irregular – 'vertices'.
- Identifying 3D shapes in everyday life can be tricky, as they are often not close enough matches to the shape (for example, milk bottles) or are compounded on to other shapes (for example, buildings).

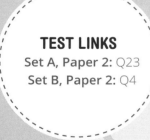

21 Patterns and sequences

Objectives

To order and arrange combinations of mathematical objects in patterns and sequences.

What the children need to know

Patterns of shapes can be created and extended.

Shapes can have different orientations as part of the patterns.

TEST LINKS
Set B, Paper 2: Q12

WORKBOOK LINKS
Pages 56–57

⌄ Support ideas

Note: Number sequences are covered in Unit 2.

- Use revision of pattern work to consolidate children's knowledge and vocabulary of 2D shapes and position/direction work (3D shape patterns are good for practice, but it is unlikely that these would occur in the national tests). Rapid and varied work can be facilitated using stickers or stamps of different shapes to create and extend patterns quickly.

- Using prepared sequences on the whiteboard, use cut and paste to show how sequences can be extended, and model how saying these aloud can help to spot the pattern. This can start with just colour (such as different colour circles in various patterns) before moving on to shapes, and then on to different-coloured shapes. For repeating sequences, draw blocks around each 'chunk' to help isolate and visualise the 'rule' – saying the rule aloud to reinforce the concept.

- Create sets of cards with different shapes on them (be sure to repeat shapes more than once – for example, include four of each shape), and challenge the children to work in small groups to turn cards over and generate sequences (starting with three shapes, then progressing to four or even five). Ask children to 'write the rule' for each sequence.

- Move on to sequences where shapes alter orientation with each stage – these are trickier in that they are not 'repeating' as in the idea above, but rather ever-changing, and if introduced carefully they can be very useful for extending thinking skills.

- Try to introduce subtle shifts in thinking skills, for example, using intersecting patterns (as in the example from the DFE sample materials shown below), to introduce greater degrees of reasoning.

⌄ Review

- Check that children are taking a systematic approach by deciding on the nature and type of the sequence before adding to it.

⌄ Beware

- Although most patterns are read from left to right, they can also be extended right to left, top to bottom and bottom to top.

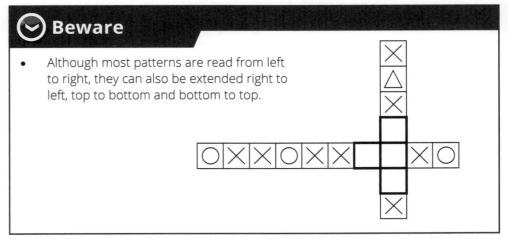

22 Position and direction

Objectives

- To use mathematical vocabulary to describe position, direction and movement, including movement in a straight line and distinguishing between rotation as a turn and in terms of right angles for quarter, half and three-quarter turns (clockwise and anti-clockwise).

What the children need to know

- How to use the language and concept of angles to describe 'turning' in terms of rotations of right angles.
- How to combine this with movement in a straight line when giving directions.

TEST LINKS
Set A, Paper 2: Q8

WORKBOOK LINKS
Pages 58–59

⌄ Support ideas

- For children struggling to grasp concepts, use a simple grid with large squares to move a figure/counter both directionally and rotationally, in single and multiple squares and by quarter turns left and right. Use flash cards with written directions on them to reinforce vocabulary in context (for example, forward, backwards, turn right) – with children moving an object on a grid.
- Use the children themselves to practise turning right and turning left. Simply standing in the classroom, ask them to turn left and right by $\frac{1}{4}$, $\frac{1}{2}$, $\frac{3}{4}$ and whole turns. Also, if desired, use an analogue clock and/or a compass to consider quarter, half, three-quarter and whole turns.
- Create simplified routes on the whiteboard, just using combinations of straight lines of different lengths and varied directions, then work with the class to write sequences of instructions to get from one end to the other. For example, go forward two blocks, make a quarter turn right, and then go forward one more block.
- Create a simplified map of a town (ideally both on the IWB and on photocopies) including icons for different shops and locations. Use this with the class to both answer and generate suggestions for different journeys that can be made, eliciting sequences of instructions for moving along the route. Challenge children further to create a sequence of journeys – a virtual shopping trip if you like!
- For children who need further support, programmable robots are still a useful support at this stage of their learning.

⌄ Review

- Ensure that children are competent both in identifying degrees of quarter-rotation in both clockwise and anti-clockwise directions.
- Also, review children's competence in sequencing instructions which combine directional movement as well as rotation, paying attention to children's vocabulary as well as their written work.

⌄ Beware

- Confusing left and right is still common at this age. Encourage the children to use their hands to help remember which is which if needs be – holding up the left hand, palm outwards with thumb outstretched, the thumb and index finger make the letter 'L' shape for left).
- The above concern also extends to remembering clockwise and anti-clockwise. Right/clockwise and left/anti-clockwise can work, as can simply visualising an analogue clock's movements.

23

Tally charts and tables

Objectives

To interpret and construct tally charts and simple tables.

To ask and answer simple questions by counting the number of objects in each category and sorting the categories by quantity.

To ask and answer questions about totalling and comparing categorical data.

What the children need to know

How to read and represent data in tables using numerals or tallies – lines constructed in sets of five using a five-bar gate approach.

Data can be used to draw conclusions, comparisons and other relevant information.

TEST LINKS
Set A, Paper 2: Q23

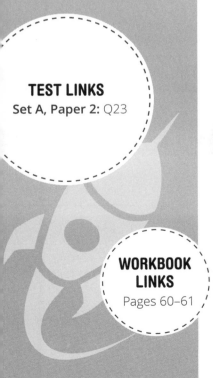

WORKBOOK LINKS
Pages 60–61

Support ideas

- Note that the ideas below for reinforcing children's understanding of tables and tally charts can often be used alongside each other, converting the tally charts to number-based tables, and vice versa.

- Using a simple show of hands, ask simple questions about preferred drinks or snacks, and generate ad-hoc tables. Use this to model both table construction as well as the relevant terms – headings, columns, rows and so on and extend this to simple questions about the data (for example, *Which is the most popular drink?*), extending to comparison of data (for example, *How many people prefer snack x to snack y?*)

- Discuss checking activities with the class. For example, if there are 30 children in the class we know that the numbers must add up to 30. This is a useful check of accuracy.

- Use children's hands to practise tally-chart construction, counting to five using their fingers for one to four, and placing the thumb across the palm/fingers for five. Discuss the merit of tallies as a way of easily keeping count during a survey.

- For counting beyond ten, demonstrate how to count and draw bars simultaneously, with the fifth item going across in the 'five-bar gate' style, and the next set of five starting separately. Show how items that do not total five are dealt with.

- Look at existing sets of tallies and work with children on totalling them. This should involve counting in fives, plus any additional tallies. To reinforce this, write the number 5 above each tally, then add the fives separately.

- Construct tally charts based around the class – for example, eye colour, pet ownership and siblings. With enough data generated for any one aspect, challenge the class to answer and also pose questions about the data, moving from simply counting totals to comparing quantities (for example, *Which is the most popular pet?*) on to more complex comparisons that involve arithmetic (for example, *How many more children have blue eyes than have brown?*) all the while introducing and modelling relevant vocabulary.

Review

- Check that children are comfortable with both constructing and reading tables and tally charts, and can convert between the two.

- Ensure that children can use data to draw conclusions, both in sorting by quantity and by totalling and comparing data.

Beware

- Children can lose their place counting tally charts. Writing a '5' above each set of bars can help avoid this, as well as counting in fives using a finger to move along each group.

Block diagrams and pictograms

Objectives

- To interpret and construct simple pictograms and block diagrams.
- To ask and answer simple questions by counting the number of objects in each category and sorting the categories by quantity.
- To ask and answer questions about totalling and comparing categorical data.

What the children need to know

- Pictograms and block diagrams help us to read data more easily.
- How to construct and interpret pictograms and bar charts.
- How to ask and answer pertinent questions about the data, as well as totalling and comparing data from different categories.

TEST LINKS
Set A, Paper 2: Q22
Set B, Paper 2: Q24

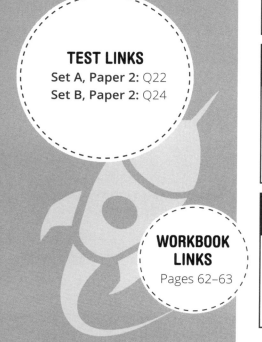

WORKBOOK LINKS
Pages 62–63

⌄ Support ideas

- Note that you can re-use data gathered in reviewing children's understanding of tables and tally charts in the previous unit to construct pictograms and block graphs. Although children may be familiar with the data, this is still valuable practice – they might look at how the intervals on the vertical axis can be varied for other than 1-to-1 correspondence for the pictograms (see below).
- With suitable data in place, try to collate digital images (for example, simple side-on views of cars) that can be used to construct large-scale pictograms on the whiteboard. Work with the class to check that the data has been accurately represented.
- Convert back and forth between pictograms (ideally using a software graphing package) and block diagrams for the same set of data, discussing the merits of each approach.
- Present the class with a block diagram or a pictogram, ideally on a large permanent display, and present questions about the information, moving on to children creating their own questions, in particular looking at the comparison of different categories including the arithmetic of totals and differences.
- The above activity should be repeated in various guises (for example, counting cars, farm animals, children's pets, favourite foods) using different correspondences for the data representation (1-to-1, 2-to-1, 5-to-1 and 10-to-1). There are ample opportunities here to reinforce counting in ones, twos, fives, and tens as in children's counting and times-tables work.
- For children struggling, use coloured blocks to construct physical block diagrams, focusing on the 1-to-1 representation of each block. This can be extended to pictograms by sticking icons onto the blocks before stacking them.

⌄ Review

- Check that children can read block diagrams easily, and review their understanding of pictograms with 1-to-many correspondences on the vertical axis.
- Can children interpret and manipulate the data, making simple calculations and drawing logical conclusions?

⌄ Beware

- The most obvious source of error is misinterpreting (or simply ignoring/forgetting) a 1-to-many correspondence in pictograms. Use numbers drawn on each item in the pictogram to reinforce this feature. Note that at this age block diagrams tend to be 1-to-1 but this should not be assumed and the same care taken in analysing them.

1. UNDERSTANDING NUMBERS

kills check. Can you?

- Identify 10s and 1s in two-digit numbers.
- Identify numbers using objects, numerals and number lines.

he knowledge

- Numbers can be used to state how many objects can be counted. 20 cakes and 20 birds are very different, but the thing they have in common is how many there are.

- Number lines are usually shown from left to right, increasing in equal steps. A ruler is a number line that starts at zero and increases in ones.
- Numbers up to 99 are written in tens and ones.

xamples

- There are 12 cubes in the circle.
- There are thirty-one pencils in the square.
- The ruler shows a number line.
- The two-digit number is seventy-six.

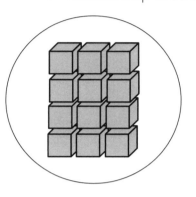

Tens	Ones
7	6

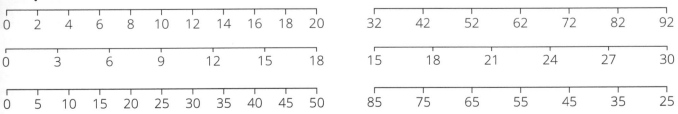

0 1 2 3 4 5 6 7 8 9 10 11 12 13 14 15

2. COUNTING IN STEPS

kills check. Can you?

- Count forwards in 2s from zero.
- Count forwards in 3s from zero.

- Count forwards in 5s from zero.
- Count forwards and backwards in 10s from any number.

he knowledge

- Counting in steps means increasing or decreasing by the same number each time.
- Counting on starting at zero is easier, but we can practise counting on from any number using a number line or a 100-square.
- Counting back can be harder, so use a number line or square to help.

xamples

| 0 | 2 | 4 | 6 | 8 | 10 | 12 | 14 | 16 | 18 | 20 |

| 32 | 42 | 52 | 62 | 72 | 82 | 92 |

| 0 | 3 | 6 | 9 | 12 | 15 | 18 |

| 15 | 18 | 21 | 24 | 27 | 30 |

| 0 | 5 | 10 | 15 | 20 | 25 | 30 | 35 | 40 | 45 | 50 |

| 85 | 75 | 65 | 55 | 45 | 35 | 25 |

3. COMPARING AND ORDERING NUMBERS

Skills check. Can you?
- Arrange numbers in order, getting larger or smaller.
- Compare numbers using less than (<), more than (>) and equals (=) signs.

The knowledge
- The size of 2-digit numbers is shown by the tens, then the ones.
- To decide which sign to use for more than or less than, remember the bigger number always goes at the wide end. Think of a crocodile with a wide open mouth eating the bigger number.

Examples
- In increasing order: 2, 7, 12, 15, 32, 39, 70, 99
- In decreasing order: 99, 70, 39, 32, 15, 12, 7, 2
- 34 > 23
- 75 < 91
- 25 = 20 and 5

4. READING AND WRITING NUMBERS

Skills check. Can you?
- Read numbers in digits and in words.
- Write numbers in digits and in words.

The knowledge
- Numbers are written in digits, using tens and ones
- We use a hyphen for numbers in words that use tens and ones, for example, 'twenty-one'.

Examples

Words	six	thirteen	twenty	twenty-one	twenty-six
Digits	6	13	20	21	26

5. SOLVING PROBLEMS WITH PLACE VALUE AND NUMBER FACTS

Skills check. Can you?
- Solve problems by counting on or back in steps.
- Solve problems using place value and number facts to add and subtract numbers.

The knowledge
- We can group objects and count the groups to solve problems, such as pairs of shoes, packs of pencils, groups of 3, and so on.
- Sometimes adding and subtracting is easier by partitioning numbers.

Examples
- 6 pairs of shoes means that there are 12 shoes.
- 7 packs of 10 pencils means there are 70 pencils. If we take 3 packs away, there are 40 pencils.
- If there are 4 packs of 10 pencils, and a child removes 3 pencils from one pack, how many will be left? $40 - 3 = 37$
- There are 23 pieces of popcorn in a bucket and Tim eats 13 of them. How many pieces are left? $23 = 13 + 10$, so there will be 10 pieces of popcorn left.

6. ADDING AND SUBTRACTING

Skills check. Can you?
- Add and subtract 1- and 2-digit numbers.
- Add and subtract two 2-digit numbers.
- Add three 1-digit numbers.
- Use pictures, objects, number lines and mental methods.

The knowledge
- We can add and subtract using objects, pictures, number lines and also mentally.
- When we add and subtract ones, we change the ones column.
- When we add and subtract tens, we change the tens column.
- If two or more 1-digit numbers add up to more than ten we must count on beyond ten.

Examples
- $6 + 3 = 9$; $7 + 5 = 12$; $13 + 5 = 18$; $5 + 13 = 18$
- $9 - 6 = 3$; $12 - 7 = 5$; $18 - 5 = 13$; $13 - 5 = 8$
- $12 + 13 = 25$; $25 + 31 = 56$
- $25 - 13 = 12$; $56 - 25 = 31$
- $1 + 2 + 3 = 6$; $4 + 5 + 6 = 15$; $7 + 8 + 9 = 24$

7. USING ADDITION AND SUBTRACTION

Skills check. Can you?

- Recall addition and subtraction facts to 20.
- Use number facts to 20 to add and subtract up to 100.
- Show that numbers can be added in any order, but not subtracted.
- Use inverse calculations to check answers and solve missing number problems.

The knowledge

- If we know a fact to 20, we can easily extend it to 100.
- We can use number squares and number lines to help us.
- Partitioning can make addition and subtraction of larger numbers easier.
- Sum is the added total of two numbers.
- Difference is the subtraction of the smaller from the bigger number.
- We get the same answer no matter what order we add numbers.
- If we change the order in which we subtract two numbers, the answer will change.
- Subtraction is the inverse of addition.

Examples

- 4 + 1 = 5, so 44 +11 = 55; 6 + 3 = 9, so 66 + 33 = 99
- 2 + 3 = 5, so 32 + 43 = 30 + 2 + 40 + 3 = 75
- 9 + 7 = 16, so 39 + 27 = 30 + 9 + 20 + 7 = 50 + 16 = 66
- 12 + 8 = 20, but 12 – 8 = 4
- 33 + 25 = 58, but 33 – 25 = 8
- 12 + 8 = 20, so 20 – 8 = 12, and 20 – 12 = 8

8. SOLVING PROBLEMS WITH ADDITION AND SUBTRACTION

Skills check. Can you?

- Use objects, pictures and numbers to solve problems using addition and subtraction.
- Use mental and written methods to solve addition and subtraction problems.

The knowledge

- Problems can involve adding and subtracting numbers of objects.
- Problems involving larger numbers can be solved using mental and written methods.

Examples

- A grocer puts 5 apples into a bag, and then another 3. How many apples are in the bag altogether?
  5 + 3 = 8

- Angie takes the bag of apples and eats 2 of them. How many apples are left?
  8 – 2 = 6
- 23 children are in a playground, and another 19 arrive. How many children are there now?
  23 + 19 = 42 children
- 30 children then go for their lunch. How many children are left behind?
  42 – 30 = 12 children

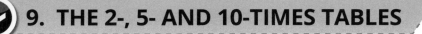

9. THE 2-, 5- AND 10-TIMES TABLES

Skills check. Can you?

- Use multiplication and division facts for the 2-times table.
- Use multiplication and division facts for the 5-times table.
- Use multiplication and division facts for the 10-times table.
- Recognise odd and even numbers.

The knowledge

- Each multiplication fact gives us three other facts (for example, $2 \times 3 = 6$; $3 \times 2 = 6$; $6 \div 3 = 2$; $6 \div 2 = 3$).
- The 2-times, 5-times and 10-times tables have several facts in common (for example, $2 \times 5 = 10$, $5 \times 2 = 10$, $1 \times 10 = 10$ etc).
- Even numbers end in 0, 2, 4, 6 and 8.
- Odd numbers end in 1, 3, 5, 7 and 9.

Examples

- $2 \times 5 = 10$; $5 \times 2 = 10$; $10 \div 5 = 2$; $10 \div 2 = 5$
- 5, 29, 47, 83 and 91 are all odd numbers.
- 6, 32, 64, 70 and 98 are all even numbers.

10. USING MULTIPLICATION AND DIVISION

Skills check. Can you?

- Write multiplication and division calculations using x and ÷ for numbers in the multiplication tables.
- Show that numbers can be multiplied in any order, but they cannot be divided in any order.
- Use inverse calculations to check work.

The knowledge

- The × and ÷ signs can be used in mathematical sentences (for example, $2 \times 3 = 6$, $6 \div 3 = 2$).
- Multiplication is commutative (for example, $2 \times 3 = 6$, $3 \times 2 = 6$).
- Division is not commutative (for example, $6 \div 3 = 2$, but $3 \div 6$ does not equal 2).

Examples

- $8 \times 2 = 16$; $5 \times 9 = 45$; $6 \times 10 = 60$
- $8 \div 2 = 4$; $30 \div 5 = 6$; $90 \div 10 = 9$
- $5 \times 10 = 50$ and $10 \times 5 = 50$; $6 \times 2 = 12$ and $2 \times 6 = 12$
- $35 \div 5 = 7$, but $5 \div 35$ does not equal 7.

11. SOLVING PROBLEMS WITH MULTIPLICATION AND DIVISION

Skills check. Can you?

- Solve multiplication problems, using known facts, materials and arrays, repeated addition and mental methods.
- Solve division problems, using known facts, materials, arrays and mental methods.
- Use inverse calculations to check work.

The knowledge

- Equipment and arrays (for example, 3 rows of 10 objects = 30 objects) can be useful to help us solve problems.
- Repeated addition is the same as multiplication.
- Division and multiplication facts are related (we say division is the inverse of multiplication).

Examples

- 3 rows of carrots with 5 carrots in each row equals 15 carrots altogether.
- If there are 80 cabbages altogether, and there are 10 cabbages per row, there must be 8 rows of cabbages.
- If there are six pairs of shoes in a shop window, how many shoes are there altogether?
  $6 \times 2 = 12$ shoes

12. RECOGNISING FRACTIONS

Skills check. Can you?

- Name and write simple fractions.
- Recognise the equivalence of $\frac{2}{4} = \frac{1}{2}$.
- Recognise and find fractions of lengths and shapes.
- Recognise and find fractions of sets of objects or quantities.

The knowledge

- Fractions you must know are $\frac{1}{4}, \frac{1}{3}, \frac{2}{4}, \frac{3}{4}$.
- Remember that $\frac{2}{4}$ is the same as $\frac{1}{2}$.
- All of these fractions can be shown using drawings of lines, shapes and objects.

Examples

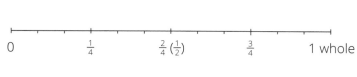

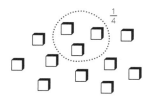

13. USING FRACTIONS

Skills check. Can you?
- Write simple fractions of whole numbers.

The knowledge
- Half of a number is the same as dividing it by 2.
- A quarter is the same as splitting a group into 4 equal parts.
- Three quarters is 3 of the 4 equal parts.
- Counting in fractions can be done on a number line.

Examples
- $\frac{1}{2}$ of 8 = 4
- $\frac{1}{4}$ of 8 = 2
- $\frac{1}{3}$ of 12 = 4
- $\frac{3}{4}$ of 8 = 6
- $\frac{1}{2}$, 1, 1 $\frac{1}{2}$, 2, 2 $\frac{1}{2}$, 3, 3 $\frac{1}{2}$, 4 ...

14. LENGTH AND TEMPERATURE

Skills check. Can you?
- Measure height and length in any direction (m and cm).
- Choose the correct units to show your measurement.
- Estimate and measure temperature using the correct units (degrees centigrade).

The knowledge
- We can use rulers to draw and measure straight lines.
- We can measure larger lengths with tape measures.
- We measure small lengths in centimetres (cm), and larger lengths in metres (m).
- Water turns to ice at 0°C, and boils at 100°C.
- A glass of water will be around 7°C.

Examples
- This toy car is 5cm long.

- This line is 2cm long.

- This desk is 1m high. 1m

- The temperature outside is 19°C.

- This cup of tea is 45°C.

15. MASS AND CAPACITY

Skills check. Can you?
- Estimate and measure mass using the correct units (grams or kilograms).
- Estimate and measure capacity using the correct units (millilitres or litres).

The knowledge
- There are 1000g in a kilogram.
- A feather weighs a few grams, a bag of sugar can weigh a kilogram.
- There are 1000ml in a litre.
- Milk is often sold in 1-l plastic bottles.
- A cup of juice is around 100 to 200ml.

Examples

- This pencil weighs 40g.

- The capacity of this cup is 200ml.

- This child weighs 35kg.

- This bottle can hold 2 l.

16. COMPARING MEASURES

Skills check. Can you?
- Compare and order different lengths.
- Compare and order different masses.
- Compare and order different capacities.
- Use >, < and = correctly.

The knowledge
- To compare two quantities we must use the same units.
- = means 'equals'.
- > means 'greater than'.
- < means 'less than'.
- We can also compare quantities using language, such as 'half as tall', 'twice as heavy'.

Examples
- 6cm > 5cm , 74m < 91m
- 3 l > 2 l , 95ml < 100ml
- 65kg > 59kg , 89g > 85g

17. MONEY

Skills check. Can you?

- Read and write different amounts of money using the '£' and 'p' symbols for pounds and pence.
- Combine different amounts of coins to make different totals.
- Solve money problems, including giving change, using addition and subtraction.

The knowledge

- There are coins for 1p, 2p, 5p, 10p, 20p, 50p, £1 and £2. We can use different numbers of these coins together to make different amounts.
- There are 100p in £1.
- We can add and subtract money just like other numbers.

Examples

- We can use one 10p and two 5ps to make 20p, or we can just use a 20p piece.
- If apples cost 5p and oranges cost 6p, three apples and two oranges will cost 15p + 12p = 27p
- If I buy a book for 80p and hand over £1, I will get 100 − 80 = 20p change.

18. TIME

Skills check. Can you?

- Compare and order different amounts of time.
- Tell and write the time to the nearest five minutes.
- Identify quarter to, quarter past and half past.
- Say the number of minutes in an hour, and the number of hours in a day.

The knowledge

- There are 60 seconds in a minute.
- There are 60 minutes in an hour.
- There are 24 hours in a day.
- There are rules for how we read a clock. The long hand shows minutes, the short hand shows hours.
- The face of a clock shows 12 hours. Each hour is divided into sections of 5 minutes.

Examples

nine o'clock   half past two   quarter to seven   midnight

- Notice how the hour hand moves just a little between each hour. It will always be after the number if the time is after the o'clock, or 'past'; and before the next number if the time is before o'clock, or 'to'.

19. 2D SHAPES

Skills check. Can you?

- Identify different 2D shapes.
- Describe shapes by their sides and their symmetry.
- Compare and sort 2D shapes and everyday objects.

The knowledge

- A regular shape has all sides the same length.
- Shapes are often symmetrical – each half is the mirror image of the other.
- A circle has one curved side.

Shape	Triangle	Square	Pentagon	Hexagon	Octagon	Circle
Number of sides	3	4	5	6	8	1

- We can sort shapes and objects by their properties.

Examples

 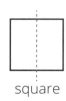

triangle   square   pentagon   hexagon   octagon   circle

- Notice that each shape has a vertical line of symmetry.

20. 3D SHAPES

Skills check. Can you?

- Identify and describe different 3D shapes.
- Identify 2D shapes on the surface of 3D shapes.
- Compare and sort 3D shapes and everyday objects.

The knowledge

- 3D shapes have edges, faces and vertices.
- Each face of a 3D shape is a particular 2D shape, except for a sphere.
- A sphere has one curved face.

Examples

Shape	Cube	Cuboid	Cone	Cylinder	Triangular prism	Square-based pyramid	Sphere
Number of edges	12	12	1	2	9	8	0
Example							
Number of faces	6	6	2	3	5	5	1
Number of vertices	8	8	0	0	6	5	0
2D shapes on faces	Squares	Squares or rectangles	Circle	Circles	Triangle and rectangles	Square and triangles	

- Don't worry about learning these facts, just learn how to identify them.

21. PATTERNS AND SEQUENCES

Skills check. Can you?

- Identify and explain patterns and sequences of mathematical objects.
- Order and arrange objects and shapes in patterns and sequences.

The knowledge

- We can create patterns and sequences by organising shapes and objects in different combinations.
- To spot a pattern, there must be at least two repeating sets of shapes or objects.
- Some patterns involve objects changing their position.

Examples

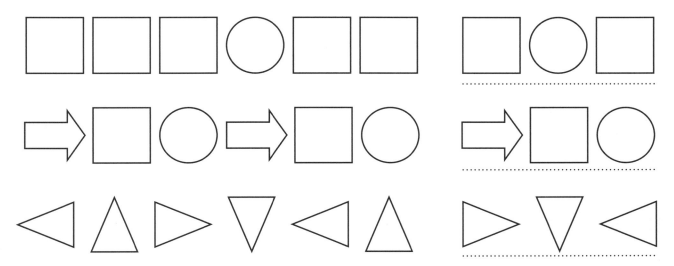

22. POSITION AND DIRECTION

Skills check. Can you?

- Describe position, direction and movement using mathematical vocabulary.
- Describe rotation in right angles for quarter, half and three-quarter turns.

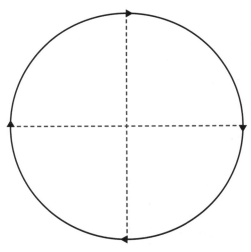

The knowledge

- We can give directions by instructions.
- We can say 'turn left' or 'turn right'.
- We can also turn in right angles, clockwise or anti-clockwise.

Examples

- Go three squares straight ahead, then turn 90° clockwise.
- Start at the shop. Walk straight down the road; turn left at the junction; continue walking and the post office is on the right.

23. TALLY CHARTS AND TABLES

Skills check. Can you?

- Understand and make tally charts.
- Understand and make simple tables.
- Ask and answer questions using tally charts.
- Ask and answer questions using tables.

The knowledge

- Tally charts help us to count data in groups of five. We call these five-bar gates.
- Tables record total numbers counted.
- Tally charts and tables need to be presented neatly to make them easy to read.

Examples

- The tally chart tells us there were more birds than cats, and more cats than dogs.
- Altogether twenty-two animals were spotted.

Animals seen on a walk	**Tally count**
Dogs	IIII
Cats	卌 I
Birds	卌 卌 II
Total animals spotted	22

- We could show the final tally chart as a table.

Animals seen on a walk	**Totals**
Dogs	4
Cats	6
Birds	12
Total animals spotted	22

24. BLOCK DIAGRAMS AND PICTOGRAMS

Skills check. Can you?

- Understand and make pictograms.
- Understand and make block diagrams.
- Ask and answer questions using pictograms.
- Ask and answer questions using block diagrams.

The knowledge

- Pictograms use icons, or symbols, to represent each object.
- Bar charts are similar to pictograms, but use a solid bar.
- You must label each axis of the graph carefully so that others can read them.

Examples

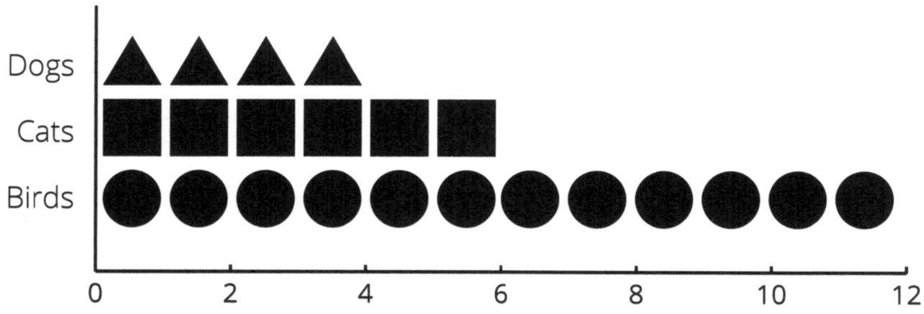

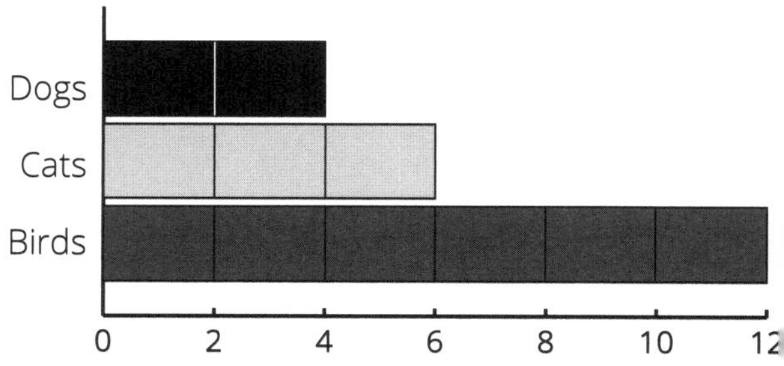

- Notice that the bar chart uses one square for every two animals counted.